THE ULTIMATE NORTH CAROLINA STATE PARKS JOURNAL

THIS JOURNAL BELONGS TO

NAME	
PHONE	
EMAIL	
ADDRESS	
NOTES	

NCPARKS.GOV

CAROLINA BEACH STATE PARK

DATE(S) VISITED

☐ FIRST VISIT ☐ RETURN VISIT

PASSPORT STAMP

TRAVEL PARTNERS

LODGING

☐ RV ☐ CABIN ☐ TENT ☐ DAY TRIP

WEATHER

FEE(S)

☐ FEE(S) ☐ FREE

SIGHTS VISITED/ACTIVITIES

WILDLIFE

HIKES

☐
☐
☐
☐
☐
☐

OVERALL EXPERIENCE

CARVERS CREEK STATE PARK

DATE(S) VISITED

☐ FIRST VISIT ☐ RETURN VISIT

PASSPORT STAMP

TRAVEL PARTNERS

LODGING

☐ RV ☐ CABIN ☐ TENT ☐ DAY TRIP

WEATHER

FEE(S)

☐ FEE(S) ☐ FREE

SIGHTS VISITED/ACTIVITIES

WILDLIFE

HIKES

☐
☐
☐

☐
☐
☐

OVERALL EXPERIENCE

CHIMNEY ROCK STATE PARK

DATE(S) VISITED

☐ FIRST VISIT   ☐ RETURN VISIT

PASSPORT STAMP

TRAVEL PARTNERS

LODGING

☐ RV   ☐ CABIN   ☐ TENT   ☐ DAY TRIP

WEATHER

FEE(S)

☐ FEE(S)   ☐ FREE

SIGHTS VISITED/ACTIVITIES

WILDLIFE

HIKES

☐   ☐

☐   ☐

☐   ☐

OVERALL EXPERIENCE

CLIFFS OF THE NEUSE STATE PARK

DATE(S) VISITED

☐ FIRST VISIT   ☐ RETURN VISIT

PASSPORT STAMP

TRAVEL PARTNERS

LODGING

☐ RV   ☐ CABIN   ☐ TENT   ☐ DAY TRIP

WEATHER

FEE(S)

☐ FEE(S)   ☐ FREE

SIGHTS VISITED/ACTIVITIES

WILDLIFE

HIKES

]	☐
]	☐
]	☐

OVERALL EXPERIENCE

CROWDERS MOUNTAIN STATE PARK

DATE(S) VISITED

☐ FIRST VISIT ☐ RETURN VISIT

PASSPORT STAMP

TRAVEL PARTNERS

LODGING

☐ RV ☐ CABIN ☐ TENT ☐ DAY TRIP

WEATHER

FEE(S)

☐ FEE(S) ☐ FREE

SIGHTS VISITED/ACTIVITIES

WILDLIFE

HIKES

☐
☐
☐

OVERALL EXPERIENCE

DISMAL SWAMP STATE PARK

DATE(S) VISITED

☐ FIRST VISIT   ☐ RETURN VISIT

PASSPORT STAMP

TRAVEL PARTNERS

LODGING

☐ RV   ☐ CABIN   ☐ TENT   ☐ DAY TRIP

WEATHER

FEE(S)

☐ FEE(S)   ☐ FREE

SIGHTS VISITED/ACTIVITIES

WILDLIFE

HIKES

	☐
	☐
	☐

OVERALL EXPERIENCE

ELK KNOB STATE PARK

DATE(S) VISITED

☐ FIRST VISIT   ☐ RETURN VISIT

PASSPORT STAMP

TRAVEL PARTNERS

LODGING

☐ RV   ☐ CABIN   ☐ TENT   ☐ DAY TRIP

WEATHER

FEE(S)

☐ FEE(S)   ☐ FREE

SIGHTS VISITED/ACTIVITIES

WILDLIFE

HIKES

☐
☐
☐
☐
☐
☐

OVERALL EXPERIENCE

ENO RIVER STATE PARK

DATE(S) VISITED

☐ FIRST VISIT   ☐ RETURN VISIT

PASSPORT STAMP

TRAVEL PARTNERS

LODGING

☐ RV   ☐ CABIN   ☐ TENT   ☐ DAY TRIP

WEATHER

FEE(S)

☐ FEE(S)   ☐ FREE

SIGHTS VISITED/ACTIVITIES

WILDLIFE

HIKES

☐
☐
☐

☐
☐
☐

OVERALL EXPERIENCE

FALLS LAKE STATE RECREATION AREA

DATE(S) VISITED

☐ FIRST VISIT   ☐ RETURN VISIT

PASSPORT STAMP

TRAVEL PARTNERS

LODGING

☐ RV   ☐ CABIN   ☐ TENT   ☐ DAY TRIP

WEATHER

FEE(S)

☐ FEE(S)   ☐ FREE

SIGHTS VISITED/ACTIVITIES

WILDLIFE

HIKES

☐
☐
☐

☐
☐
☐

OVERALL EXPERIENCE

FORT FISHER STATE RECREATION AREA

DATE(S) VISITED

☐ FIRST VISIT   ☐ RETURN VISIT

PASSPORT STAMP

TRAVEL PARTNERS

LODGING

☐ RV   ☐ CABIN   ☐ TENT   ☐ DAY TRIP

WEATHER

FEE(S)

☐ FEE(S)   ☐ FREE

SIGHTS VISITED/ACTIVITIES

WILDLIFE

HIKES

☐

☐

☐

OVERALL EXPERIENCE

FORT MACON STATE PARK

DATE(S) VISITED

☐ FIRST VISIT   ☐ RETURN VISIT

PASSPORT STAMP

TRAVEL PARTNERS

LODGING

☐ RV   ☐ CABIN   ☐ TENT   ☐ DAY TRIP

WEATHER

FEE(S)

☐ FEE(S)   ☐ FREE

SIGHTS VISITED/ACTIVITIES

WILDLIFE

HIKES

☐
☐
☐

☐
☐
☐

OVERALL EXPERIENCE

GOOSE CREEK STATE PARK

DATE(S) VISITED

☐ FIRST VISIT   ☐ RETURN VISIT

PASSPORT STAMP

TRAVEL PARTNERS

LODGING

☐ RV   ☐ CABIN   ☐ TENT   ☐ DAY TRIP

WEATHER

FEE(S)

☐ FEE(S)   ☐ FREE

SIGHTS VISITED/ACTIVITIES

WILDLIFE

HIKES

	☐
	☐
	☐

OVERALL EXPERIENCE

GORGES STATE PARK

DATE(S) VISITED

☐ FIRST VISIT   ☐ RETURN VISIT

PASSPORT STAMP

TRAVEL PARTNERS

LODGING

☐ RV   ☐ CABIN   ☐ TENT   ☐ DAY TRIP

WEATHER

FEE(S)

☐ FEE(S)   ☐ FREE

SIGHTS VISITED/ACTIVITIES

WILDLIFE

HIKES

☐   ☐
☐   ☐
☐   ☐

OVERALL EXPERIENCE

GRANDFATHER MOUNTAIN STATE PARK

DATE(S) VISITED

☐ FIRST VISIT   ☐ RETURN VISIT

PASSPORT STAMP

TRAVEL PARTNERS

LODGING

☐ RV   ☐ CABIN   ☐ TENT   ☐ DAY TRIP

WEATHER

FEE(S)

☐ FEE(S)   ☐ FREE

SIGHTS VISITED/ACTIVITIES

WILDLIFE

HIKES

☐
☐
☐

☐
☐
☐

OVERALL EXPERIENCE

HAMMOCKS BEACH STATE PARK

DATE(S) VISITED

☐ FIRST VISIT   ☐ RETURN VISIT

PASSPORT STAMP

TRAVEL PARTNERS

LODGING

☐ RV   ☐ CABIN   ☐ TENT   ☐ DAY TRIP

WEATHER

FEE(S)

☐ FEE(S)   ☐ FREE

SIGHTS VISITED/ACTIVITIES

WILDLIFE

HIKES

☐
☐
☐
☐
☐
☐

OVERALL EXPERIENCE

HANGING ROCK STATE PARK

DATE(S) VISITED

☐ FIRST VISIT   ☐ RETURN VISIT

PASSPORT STAMP

TRAVEL PARTNERS

LODGING

☐ RV   ☐ CABIN   ☐ TENT   ☐ DAY TRIP

WEATHER

FEE(S)

☐ FEE(S)   ☐ FREE

SIGHTS VISITED/ACTIVITIES

WILDLIFE

HIKES

☐

☐

☐

OVERALL EXPERIENCE

HAW RIVER STATE PARK

DATE(S) VISITED

☐ FIRST VISIT   ☐ RETURN VISIT

PASSPORT STAMP

TRAVEL PARTNERS

LODGING

☐ RV   ☐ CABIN   ☐ TENT   ☐ DAY TRIP

WEATHER

FEE(S)

☐ FEE(S)   ☐ FREE

SIGHTS VISITED/ACTIVITIES

WILDLIFE

HIKES

☐
☐
☐

☐
☐
☐

OVERALL EXPERIENCE

JOCKEY'S RIDGE STATE PARK

DATE(S) VISITED

☐ FIRST VISIT   ☐ RETURN VISIT

PASSPORT STAMP

TRAVEL PARTNERS

LODGING

☐ RV   ☐ CABIN   ☐ TENT   ☐ DAY TRIP

WEATHER

FEE(S)

☐ FEE(S)   ☐ FREE

SIGHTS VISITED/ACTIVITIES

WILDLIFE

HIKES

☐
☐
☐

OVERALL EXPERIENCE

JONES LAKE STATE PARK

DATE(S) VISITED

☐ FIRST VISIT ☐ RETURN VISIT

PASSPORT STAMP

TRAVEL PARTNERS

LODGING

☐ RV ☐ CABIN ☐ TENT ☐ DAY TRIP

WEATHER

FEE(S)

☐ FEE(S) ☐ FREE

SIGHTS VISITED/ACTIVITIES

WILDLIFE

HIKES

☐
☐
☐

☐
☐
☐

OVERALL EXPERIENCE

JORDAN LAKE STATE RECREATION AREA

DATE(S) VISITED

☐ FIRST VISIT ☐ RETURN VISIT

PASSPORT STAMP

TRAVEL PARTNERS

LODGING

☐ RV ☐ CABIN ☐ TENT ☐ DAY TRIP

WEATHER

FEE(S)

☐ FEE(S) ☐ FREE

SIGHTS VISITED/ACTIVITIES

WILDLIFE

HIKES

☐
☐
☐

☐
☐
☐

OVERALL EXPERIENCE

KERR LAKE STATE RECREATION AREA

DATE(S) VISITED

☐ FIRST VISIT   ☐ RETURN VISIT

PASSPORT STAMP

TRAVEL PARTNERS

LODGING

☐ RV   ☐ CABIN   ☐ TENT   ☐ DAY TRIP

WEATHER

FEE(S)

☐ FEE(S)   ☐ FREE

SIGHTS VISITED/ACTIVITIES

WILDLIFE

HIKES

☐
☐
☐

☐
☐
☐

OVERALL EXPERIENCE

LAKE JAMES STATE PARK

DATE(S) VISITED

☐ FIRST VISIT　　☐ RETURN VISIT

PASSPORT STAMP

TRAVEL PARTNERS

LODGING

☐ RV　　☐ CABIN　　☐ TENT　　☐ DAY TRIP

WEATHER

FEE(S)

☐ FEE(S)　　　　　　　　　☐ FREE

SIGHTS VISITED/ACTIVITIES

WILDLIFE

HIKES

	☐
	☐
	☐

OVERALL EXPERIENCE

LAKE NORMAN STATE PARK

DATE(S) VISITED

☐ FIRST VISIT   ☐ RETURN VISIT

PASSPORT STAMP

TRAVEL PARTNERS

LODGING

☐ RV   ☐ CABIN   ☐ TENT   ☐ DAY TRIP

WEATHER

FEE(S)

☐ FEE(S)   ☐ FREE

SIGHTS VISITED/ACTIVITIES

WILDLIFE

HIKES

☐
☐
☐

☐
☐
☐

OVERALL EXPERIENCE

LAKE WACCAMAW STATE PARK

DATE(S) VISITED

☐ FIRST VISIT   ☐ RETURN VISIT

PASSPORT STAMP

TRAVEL PARTNERS

LODGING

☐ RV   ☐ CABIN   ☐ TENT   ☐ DAY TRIP

WEATHER

FEE(S)

☐ FEE(S)   ☐ FREE

SIGHTS VISITED/ACTIVITIES

WILDLIFE

HIKES

	☐
	☐
	☐

OVERALL EXPERIENCE

LUMBER RIVER STATE PARK

DATE(S) VISITED

☐ FIRST VISIT   ☐ RETURN VISIT

PASSPORT STAMP

TRAVEL PARTNERS

LODGING

☐ RV   ☐ CABIN   ☐ TENT   ☐ DAY TRIP

WEATHER

FEE(S)

☐ FEE(S)   ☐ FREE

SIGHTS VISITED/ACTIVITIES

WILDLIFE

HIKES

☐
☐
☐
☐
☐
☐

OVERALL EXPERIENCE

MAYO RIVER STATE PARK

DATE(S) VISITED

☐ FIRST VISIT   ☐ RETURN VISIT

PASSPORT STAMP

TRAVEL PARTNERS

LODGING

☐ RV   ☐ CABIN   ☐ TENT   ☐ DAY TRIP

WEATHER

FEE(S)

☐ FEE(S)   ☐ FREE

SIGHTS VISITED/ACTIVITIES

WILDLIFE

HIKES

☐   ☐
☐   ☐
☐   ☐

OVERALL EXPERIENCE

MEDOC MOUNTAIN STATE PARK

DATE(S) VISITED

☐ FIRST VISIT   ☐ RETURN VISIT

PASSPORT STAMP

TRAVEL PARTNERS

LODGING

☐ RV   ☐ CABIN   ☐ TENT   ☐ DAY TRIP

WEATHER

FEE(S)

☐ FEE(S)   ☐ FREE

SIGHTS VISITED/ACTIVITIES

WILDLIFE

HIKES

☐
☐
☐

☐
☐
☐

OVERALL EXPERIENCE

MERCHANTS MILLPOND STATE PARK

DATE(S) VISITED

☐ FIRST VISIT   ☐ RETURN VISIT

PASSPORT STAMP

TRAVEL PARTNERS

LODGING

☐ RV   ☐ CABIN   ☐ TENT   ☐ DAY TRIP

WEATHER

FEE(S)

☐ FEE(S)   ☐ FREE

SIGHTS VISITED/ACTIVITIES

WILDLIFE

HIKES

☐
☐
☐

OVERALL EXPERIENCE

MORROW MOUNTAIN STATE PARK

DATE(S) VISITED

☐ FIRST VISIT   ☐ RETURN VISIT

PASSPORT STAMP

TRAVEL PARTNERS

LODGING

☐ RV   ☐ CABIN   ☐ TENT   ☐ DAY TRIP

WEATHER

FEE(S)

☐ FEE(S)   ☐ FREE

SIGHTS VISITED/ACTIVITIES

WILDLIFE

HIKES

☐
☐
☐

☐
☐
☐

OVERALL EXPERIENCE

MOUNT JEFFERSON STATE PARK

DATE(S) VISITED

☐ FIRST VISIT   ☐ RETURN VISIT

PASSPORT STAMP

TRAVEL PARTNERS

LODGING

☐ RV   ☐ CABIN   ☐ TENT   ☐ DAY TRIP

WEATHER

FEE(S)

☐ FEE(S)   ☐ FREE

SIGHTS VISITED/ACTIVITIES

WILDLIFE

HIKES

☐

☐

☐

OVERALL EXPERIENCE

MOUNT MITCHELL STATE PARK

DATE(S) VISITED

☐ FIRST VISIT   ☐ RETURN VISIT

PASSPORT STAMP

TRAVEL PARTNERS

LODGING

☐ RV   ☐ CABIN   ☐ TENT   ☐ DAY TRIP

WEATHER

FEE(S)

☐ FEE(S)   ☐ FREE

SIGHTS VISITED/ACTIVITIES

WILDLIFE

HIKES

☐
☐
☐
☐
☐
☐

OVERALL EXPERIENCE

NEW RIVER STATE PARK

DATE(S) VISITED

☐ FIRST VISIT   ☐ RETURN VISIT

PASSPORT STAMP

TRAVEL PARTNERS

LODGING

☐ RV   ☐ CABIN   ☐ TENT   ☐ DAY TRIP

WEATHER

FEE(S)

☐ FEE(S)   ☐ FREE

SIGHTS VISITED/ACTIVITIES

WILDLIFE

HIKES

☐
☐
☐

☐
☐
☐

OVERALL EXPERIENCE

OCCONEECHEE MOUNTAIN STATE NATURAL AREA

DATE(S) VISITED

☐ FIRST VISIT   ☐ RETURN VISIT

PASSPORT STAMP

TRAVEL PARTNERS

LODGING

☐ RV   ☐ CABIN   ☐ TENT   ☐ DAY TRIP

WEATHER

FEE(S)

☐ FEE(S)   ☐ FREE

SIGHTS VISITED/ACTIVITIES

WILDLIFE

HIKES

☐
☐
☐
☐
☐
☐

OVERALL EXPERIENCE

PETTIGREW STATE PARK

DATE(S) VISITED

☐ FIRST VISIT   ☐ RETURN VISIT

PASSPORT STAMP

TRAVEL PARTNERS

LODGING

☐ RV   ☐ CABIN   ☐ TENT   ☐ DAY TRIP

WEATHER

FEE(S)

☐ FEE(S)   ☐ FREE

SIGHTS VISITED/ACTIVITIES

WILDLIFE

HIKES

☐
☐
☐

OVERALL EXPERIENCE

PILOT MOUNTAIN STATE PARK

DATE(S) VISITED

☐ FIRST VISIT   ☐ RETURN VISIT

PASSPORT STAMP

TRAVEL PARTNERS

LODGING

☐ RV   ☐ CABIN   ☐ TENT   ☐ DAY TRIP

WEATHER

FEE(S)

☐ FEE(S)   ☐ FREE

SIGHTS VISITED/ACTIVITIES

WILDLIFE

HIKES

☐
☐
☐

☐
☐
☐

OVERALL EXPERIENCE

RAVEN ROCK STATE PARK

DATE(S) VISITED

☐ FIRST VISIT   ☐ RETURN VISIT

PASSPORT STAMP

TRAVEL PARTNERS

LODGING

☐ RV   ☐ CABIN   ☐ TENT   ☐ DAY TRIP

WEATHER

FEE(S)

☐ FEE(S)   ☐ FREE

SIGHTS VISITED/ACTIVITIES

WILDLIFE

HIKES

☐

☐

☐

OVERALL EXPERIENCE

SINGLETARY LAKE STATE PARK

DATE(S) VISITED

☐ FIRST VISIT   ☐ RETURN VISIT

PASSPORT STAMP

TRAVEL PARTNERS

LODGING

☐ RV   ☐ CABIN   ☐ TENT   ☐ DAY TRIP

WEATHER

FEE(S)

☐ FEE(S)   ☐ FREE

SIGHTS VISITED/ACTIVITIES

WILDLIFE

HIKES

☐
☐
☐

☐
☐
☐

OVERALL EXPERIENCE

SOUTH MOUNTAINS STATE PARK

DATE(S) VISITED

☐ FIRST VISIT   ☐ RETURN VISIT

PASSPORT STAMP

TRAVEL PARTNERS

LODGING

☐ RV   ☐ CABIN   ☐ TENT   ☐ DAY TRIP

WEATHER

FEE(S)

☐ FEE(S)   ☐ FREE

SIGHTS VISITED/ACTIVITIES

WILDLIFE

HIKES

☐
☐
☐
☐
☐
☐

OVERALL EXPERIENCE

STONE MOUNTAIN STATE PARK

DATE(S) VISITED

☐ FIRST VISIT   ☐ RETURN VISIT

PASSPORT STAMP

TRAVEL PARTNERS

LODGING

☐ RV   ☐ CABIN   ☐ TENT   ☐ DAY TRIP

WEATHER

FEE(S)

☐ FEE(S)   ☐ FREE

SIGHTS VISITED/ACTIVITIES

WILDLIFE

HIKES

☐
☐
☐

☐
☐
☐

OVERALL EXPERIENCE

WEYMOUTH WOODS SANDHILLS NATURE PRESERVE

DATE(S) VISITED

☐ FIRST VISIT   ☐ RETURN VISIT

PASSPORT STAMP

TRAVEL PARTNERS

LODGING

☐ RV   ☐ CABIN   ☐ TENT   ☐ DAY TRIP

WEATHER

FEE(S)

☐ FEE(S)   ☐ FREE

SIGHTS VISITED/ACTIVITIES

WILDLIFE

HIKES

	☐
	☐
	☐

OVERALL EXPERIENCE

WILLIAM B. UMSTEAD STATE PARK

DATE(S) VISITED

☐ FIRST VISIT ☐ RETURN VISIT

PASSPORT STAMP

TRAVEL PARTNERS

LODGING

☐ RV ☐ CABIN ☐ TENT ☐ DAY TRIP

WEATHER

FEE(S)

☐ FEE(S) ☐ FREE

SIGHTS VISITED/ACTIVITIES

WILDLIFE

HIKES

☐
☐
☐
☐
☐
☐

OVERALL EXPERIENCE

DATE(S) VISITED

☐ FIRST VISIT ☐ RETURN VISIT

PASSPORT STAMP

TRAVEL PARTNERS

LODGING

☐ RV ☐ CABIN ☐ TENT ☐ DAY TRIP

WEATHER

FEE(S)

☐ FEE(S) ☐ FREE

SIGHTS VISITED/ACTIVITIES

WILDLIFE

HIKES

	☐
	☐
	☐

OVERALL EXPERIENCE

DATE(S) VISITED

☐ FIRST VISIT   ☐ RETURN VISIT

PASSPORT STAMP

TRAVEL PARTNERS

LODGING

☐ RV   ☐ CABIN   ☐ TENT   ☐ DAY TRIP

WEATHER

FEE(S)

☐ FEE(S)   ☐ FREE

SIGHTS VISITED/ACTIVITIES

WILDLIFE

HIKES

☐
☐
☐
☐
☐
☐

OVERALL EXPERIENCE

DATE(S) VISITED

☐ FIRST VISIT ☐ RETURN VISIT

PASSPORT STAMP

TRAVEL PARTNERS

LODGING

☐ RV ☐ CABIN ☐ TENT ☐ DAY TRIP

WEATHER

FEE(S)

☐ FEE(S) ☐ FREE

SIGHTS VISITED/ACTIVITIES

WILDLIFE

HIKES

☐
☐
☐
☐
☐
☐

OVERALL EXPERIENCE

DATE(S) VISITED

☐ FIRST VISIT   ☐ RETURN VISIT

PASSPORT STAMP

TRAVEL PARTNERS

LODGING

☐ RV   ☐ CABIN   ☐ TENT   ☐ DAY TRIP

WEATHER

FEE(S)

☐ FEE(S)   ☐ FREE

SIGHTS VISITED/ACTIVITIES

WILDLIFE

HIKES

☐
☐
☐

☐
☐
☐

OVERALL EXPERIENCE

DATE(S) VISITED

☐ FIRST VISIT   ☐ RETURN VISIT

PASSPORT STAMP

TRAVEL PARTNERS

LODGING

☐ RV   ☐ CABIN   ☐ TENT   ☐ DAY TRIP

WEATHER

FEE(S)

☐ FEE(S)   ☐ FREE

SIGHTS VISITED/ACTIVITIES

WILDLIFE

HIKES

	☐
	☐
	☐

OVERALL EXPERIENCE

DATE(S) VISITED

☐ FIRST VISIT ☐ RETURN VISIT

PASSPORT STAMP

TRAVEL PARTNERS

LODGING

☐ RV ☐ CABIN ☐ TENT ☐ DAY TRIP

WEATHER

FEE(S)

☐ FEE(S) ☐ FREE

SIGHTS VISITED/ACTIVITIES

WILDLIFE

HIKES

☐ ☐
☐ ☐
☐ ☐

OVERALL EXPERIENCE

DATE(S) VISITED

☐ FIRST VISIT   ☐ RETURN VISIT

PASSPORT STAMP

TRAVEL PARTNERS

LODGING

☐ RV   ☐ CABIN   ☐ TENT   ☐ DAY TRIP

WEATHER

FEE(S)

☐ FEE(S)   ☐ FREE

SIGHTS VISITED/ACTIVITIES

WILDLIFE

HIKES

☐
☐
☐

OVERALL EXPERIENCE

DATE(S) VISITED

☐ FIRST VISIT   ☐ RETURN VISIT

PASSPORT STAMP

TRAVEL PARTNERS

LODGING

☐ RV   ☐ CABIN   ☐ TENT   ☐ DAY TRIP

WEATHER

FEE(S)

☐ FEE(S)   ☐ FREE

SIGHTS VISITED/ACTIVITIES

WILDLIFE

HIKES

☐
☐
☐
☐
☐
☐

OVERALL EXPERIENCE

DATE(S) VISITED

☐ FIRST VISIT   ☐ RETURN VISIT

PASSPORT STAMP

TRAVEL PARTNERS

LODGING

☐ RV   ☐ CABIN   ☐ TENT   ☐ DAY TRIP

WEATHER

FEE(S)

☐ FEE(S)   ☐ FREE

SIGHTS VISITED/ACTIVITIES

WILDLIFE

HIKES

☐
☐
☐

☐
☐
☐

OVERALL EXPERIENCE

DATE(S) VISITED

☐ FIRST VISIT   ☐ RETURN VISIT

PASSPORT STAMP

TRAVEL PARTNERS

LODGING

☐ RV   ☐ CABIN   ☐ TENT   ☐ DAY TRIP

WEATHER

FEE(S)

☐ FEE(S)   ☐ FREE

SIGHTS VISITED/ACTIVITIES

WILDLIFE

HIKES

☐
☐
☐
☐
☐
☐

OVERALL EXPERIENCE

DATE(S) VISITED

☐ FIRST VISIT　　☐ RETURN VISIT

PASSPORT STAMP

TRAVEL PARTNERS

LODGING

☐ RV　　☐ CABIN　　☐ TENT　　☐ DAY TRIP

WEATHER

FEE(S)

☐ FEE(S)　　　　　　　　　　☐ FREE

SIGHTS VISITED/ACTIVITIES

WILDLIFE

HIKES

	☐
☐	☐
☐	☐
☐	☐

OVERALL EXPERIENCE

DATE(S) VISITED

☐ FIRST VISIT   ☐ RETURN VISIT

PASSPORT STAMP

TRAVEL PARTNERS

LODGING

☐ RV   ☐ CABIN   ☐ TENT   ☐ DAY TRIP

WEATHER

FEE(S)

☐ FEE(S)   ☐ FREE

SIGHTS VISITED/ACTIVITIES

WILDLIFE

HIKES

☐
☐
☐

☐
☐
☐

OVERALL EXPERIENCE

DATE(S) VISITED

☐ FIRST VISIT ☐ RETURN VISIT

PASSPORT STAMP

TRAVEL PARTNERS

LODGING

☐ RV ☐ CABIN ☐ TENT ☐ DAY TRIP

WEATHER

FEE(S)

☐ FEE(S) ☐ FREE

SIGHTS VISITED/ACTIVITIES

WILDLIFE

HIKES

☐
☐
☐

OVERALL EXPERIENCE

DATE(S) VISITED

☐ FIRST VISIT ☐ RETURN VISIT

PASSPORT STAMP

TRAVEL PARTNERS

LODGING

☐ RV ☐ CABIN ☐ TENT ☐ DAY TRIP

WEATHER

FEE(S)

☐ FEE(S) ☐ FREE

SIGHTS VISITED/ACTIVITIES

WILDLIFE

HIKES

☐
☐
☐

☐
☐
☐

OVERALL EXPERIENCE

DATE(S) VISITED

☐ FIRST VISIT   ☐ RETURN VISIT

PASSPORT STAMP

TRAVEL PARTNERS

LODGING

☐ RV   ☐ CABIN   ☐ TENT   ☐ DAY TRIP

WEATHER

FEE(S)

☐ FEE(S)   ☐ FREE

SIGHTS VISITED/ACTIVITIES

WILDLIFE

HIKES

☐
☐
☐
☐
☐
☐

OVERALL EXPERIENCE

DATE(S) VISITED

☐ FIRST VISIT ☐ RETURN VISIT

PASSPORT STAMP

TRAVEL PARTNERS

LODGING

☐ RV   ☐ CABIN   ☐ TENT   ☐ DAY TRIP

WEATHER

FEE(S)

☐ FEE(S)   ☐ FREE

SIGHTS VISITED/ACTIVITIES

WILDLIFE

HIKES

☐
☐
☐
☐
☐
☐

OVERALL EXPERIENCE

DATE(S) VISITED

☐ FIRST VISIT   ☐ RETURN VISIT

PASSPORT STAMP

TRAVEL PARTNERS

LODGING

☐ RV   ☐ CABIN   ☐ TENT   ☐ DAY TRIP

WEATHER

FEE(S)

☐ FEE(S)   ☐ FREE

SIGHTS VISITED/ACTIVITIES

WILDLIFE

HIKES

☐
☐
☐

OVERALL EXPERIENCE

DATE(S) VISITED

☐ FIRST VISIT   ☐ RETURN VISIT

PASSPORT STAMP

TRAVEL PARTNERS

LODGING

☐ RV   ☐ CABIN   ☐ TENT   ☐ DAY TRIP

WEATHER

FEE(S)

☐ FEE(S)   ☐ FREE

SIGHTS VISITED/ACTIVITIES

WILDLIFE

HIKES

☐
☐
☐
☐
☐
☐

OVERALL EXPERIENCE

DATE(S) VISITED

☐ FIRST VISIT   ☐ RETURN VISIT

PASSPORT STAMP

TRAVEL PARTNERS

LODGING

☐ RV   ☐ CABIN   ☐ TENT   ☐ DAY TRIP

WEATHER

FEE(S)

☐ FEE(S)   ☐ FREE

SIGHTS VISITED/ACTIVITIES

WILDLIFE

HIKES

☐

☐

☐

OVERALL EXPERIENCE

DATE(S) VISITED

☐ FIRST VISIT   ☐ RETURN VISIT

PASSPORT STAMP

TRAVEL PARTNERS

LODGING

☐ RV   ☐ CABIN   ☐ TENT   ☐ DAY TRIP

WEATHER

FEE(S)

☐ FEE(S)   ☐ FREE

SIGHTS VISITED/ACTIVITIES

WILDLIFE

HIKES

☐
☐
☐

☐
☐
☐

OVERALL EXPERIENCE

DATE(S) VISITED

☐ FIRST VISIT   ☐ RETURN VISIT

PASSPORT STAMP

TRAVEL PARTNERS

LODGING

☐ RV   ☐ CABIN   ☐ TENT   ☐ DAY TRIP

WEATHER

FEE(S)

☐ FEE(S)   ☐ FREE

SIGHTS VISITED/ACTIVITIES

WILDLIFE

HIKES

☐   ☐

☐   ☐

☐   ☐

OVERALL EXPERIENCE

DATE(S) VISITED

☐ FIRST VISIT   ☐ RETURN VISIT

PASSPORT STAMP

TRAVEL PARTNERS

LODGING

☐ RV   ☐ CABIN   ☐ TENT   ☐ DAY TRIP

WEATHER

FEE(S)

☐ FEE(S)   ☐ FREE

SIGHTS VISITED/ACTIVITIES

WILDLIFE

HIKES

☐
☐
☐
☐
☐
☐

OVERALL EXPERIENCE

DATE(S) VISITED

☐ FIRST VISIT   ☐ RETURN VISIT

PASSPORT STAMP

TRAVEL PARTNERS

LODGING

☐ RV   ☐ CABIN   ☐ TENT   ☐ DAY TRIP

WEATHER

FEE(S)

☐ FEE(S)   ☐ FREE

SIGHTS VISITED/ACTIVITIES

WILDLIFE

HIKES

	☐
☐	☐
	☐
	☐

OVERALL EXPERIENCE

DATE(S) VISITED

☐ FIRST VISIT   ☐ RETURN VISIT

PASSPORT STAMP

TRAVEL PARTNERS

LODGING

☐ RV   ☐ CABIN   ☐ TENT   ☐ DAY TRIP

WEATHER

FEE(S)

☐ FEE(S)   ☐ FREE

SIGHTS VISITED/ACTIVITIES

WILDLIFE

HIKES

☐
☐
☐
☐
☐
☐

OVERALL EXPERIENCE

DATE(S) VISITED

☐ FIRST VISIT   ☐ RETURN VISIT

PASSPORT STAMP

TRAVEL PARTNERS

LODGING

☐ RV   ☐ CABIN   ☐ TENT   ☐ DAY TRIP

WEATHER

FEE(S)

☐ FEE(S)   ☐ FREE

SIGHTS VISITED/ACTIVITIES

WILDLIFE

HIKES

☐
☐
☐

OVERALL EXPERIENCE

DATE(S) VISITED

☐ FIRST VISIT ☐ RETURN VISIT

PASSPORT STAMP

TRAVEL PARTNERS

LODGING

☐ RV ☐ CABIN ☐ TENT ☐ DAY TRIP

WEATHER

FEE(S)

☐ FEE(S) ☐ FREE

SIGHTS VISITED/ACTIVITIES

WILDLIFE

HIKES

☐
☐
☐

☐
☐
☐

OVERALL EXPERIENCE

DATE(S) VISITED

☐ FIRST VISIT   ☐ RETURN VISIT

PASSPORT STAMP

TRAVEL PARTNERS

LODGING

☐ RV   ☐ CABIN   ☐ TENT   ☐ DAY TRIP

WEATHER

FEE(S)

☐ FEE(S)   ☐ FREE

SIGHTS VISITED/ACTIVITIES

WILDLIFE

HIKES

☐
☐
☐

☐
☐
☐

OVERALL EXPERIENCE

DATE(S) VISITED	TRAVEL PARTNERS

DATE(S) VISITED

☐ FIRST VISIT   ☐ RETURN VISIT

PASSPORT STAMP

TRAVEL PARTNERS

LODGING

☐ RV   ☐ CABIN   ☐ TENT   ☐ DAY TRIP

WEATHER

FEE(S)

☐ FEE(S)   ☐ FREE

SIGHTS VISITED/ACTIVITIES

WILDLIFE

HIKES

☐
☐
☐

☐
☐
☐

OVERALL EXPERIENCE

DATE(S) VISITED

☐ FIRST VISIT   ☐ RETURN VISIT

PASSPORT STAMP

TRAVEL PARTNERS

LODGING

☐ RV   ☐ CABIN   ☐ TENT   ☐ DAY TRIP

WEATHER

FEE(S)

☐ FEE(S)   ☐ FREE

SIGHTS VISITED/ACTIVITIES

WILDLIFE

HIKES

☐
☐
☐

OVERALL EXPERIENCE

DATE(S) VISITED

☐ FIRST VISIT   ☐ RETURN VISIT

PASSPORT STAMP

TRAVEL PARTNERS

LODGING

☐ RV   ☐ CABIN   ☐ TENT   ☐ DAY TRIP

WEATHER

FEE(S)

☐ FEE(S)   ☐ FREE

SIGHTS VISITED/ACTIVITIES

WILDLIFE

HIKES

☐
☐
☐

☐
☐
☐

OVERALL EXPERIENCE

DATE(S) VISITED

☐ FIRST VISIT   ☐ RETURN VISIT

PASSPORT STAMP

TRAVEL PARTNERS

LODGING

☐ RV   ☐ CABIN   ☐ TENT   ☐ DAY TRIP

WEATHER

FEE(S)

☐ FEE(S)   ☐ FREE

SIGHTS VISITED/ACTIVITIES

WILDLIFE

HIKES

☐
☐
☐

OVERALL EXPERIENCE

DATE(S) VISITED

☐ FIRST VISIT   ☐ RETURN VISIT

PASSPORT STAMP

TRAVEL PARTNERS

LODGING

☐ RV   ☐ CABIN   ☐ TENT   ☐ DAY TRIP

WEATHER

FEE(S)

☐ FEE(S)   ☐ FREE

SIGHTS VISITED/ACTIVITIES

WILDLIFE

HIKES

☐
☐
☐

OVERALL EXPERIENCE

DATE(S) VISITED

☐ FIRST VISIT   ☐ RETURN VISIT

PASSPORT STAMP

TRAVEL PARTNERS

LODGING

☐ RV   ☐ CABIN   ☐ TENT   ☐ DAY TRIP

WEATHER

FEE(S)

☐ FEE(S)   ☐ FREE

SIGHTS VISITED/ACTIVITIES

WILDLIFE

HIKES

☐
☐
☐
☐
☐
☐

OVERALL EXPERIENCE

DATE(S) VISITED

☐ FIRST VISIT   ☐ RETURN VISIT

PASSPORT STAMP

TRAVEL PARTNERS

LODGING

☐ RV   ☐ CABIN   ☐ TENT   ☐ DAY TRIP

WEATHER

FEE(S)

☐ FEE(S)   ☐ FREE

SIGHTS VISITED/ACTIVITIES

WILDLIFE

HIKES

☐
☐

☐
☐

☐
☐

OVERALL EXPERIENCE

DATE(S) VISITED

☐ FIRST VISIT   ☐ RETURN VISIT

PASSPORT STAMP

TRAVEL PARTNERS

LODGING

☐ RV   ☐ CABIN   ☐ TENT   ☐ DAY TRIP

WEATHER

FEE(S)

☐ FEE(S)   ☐ FREE

SIGHTS VISITED/ACTIVITIES

WILDLIFE

HIKES

☐

☐

☐

OVERALL EXPERIENCE

DATE(S) VISITED

☐ FIRST VISIT   ☐ RETURN VISIT

PASSPORT STAMP

TRAVEL PARTNERS

LODGING

☐ RV   ☐ CABIN   ☐ TENT   ☐ DAY TRIP

WEATHER

FEE(S)

☐ FEE(S)   ☐ FREE

SIGHTS VISITED/ACTIVITIES

WILDLIFE

HIKES

☐
☐
☐
☐
☐
☐

OVERALL EXPERIENCE

DATE(S) VISITED

☐ FIRST VISIT   ☐ RETURN VISIT

PASSPORT STAMP

TRAVEL PARTNERS

LODGING

☐ RV   ☐ CABIN   ☐ TENT   ☐ DAY TRIP

WEATHER

FEE(S)

☐ FEE(S)   ☐ FREE

SIGHTS VISITED/ACTIVITIES

WILDLIFE

HIKES

	☐
	☐
	☐

OVERALL EXPERIENCE

DATE(S) VISITED

☐ FIRST VISIT   ☐ RETURN VISIT

PASSPORT STAMP

TRAVEL PARTNERS

LODGING

☐ RV   ☐ CABIN   ☐ TENT   ☐ DAY TRIP

WEATHER

FEE(S)

☐ FEE(S)   ☐ FREE

SIGHTS VISITED/ACTIVITIES

WILDLIFE

HIKES

☐
☐
☐

☐
☐
☐

OVERALL EXPERIENCE

DATE(S) VISITED	TRAVEL PARTNERS

DATE(S) VISITED

☐ FIRST VISIT   ☐ RETURN VISIT

PASSPORT STAMP

TRAVEL PARTNERS

LODGING

☐ RV   ☐ CABIN   ☐ TENT   ☐ DAY TRIP

WEATHER

FEE(S)

☐ FEE(S)   ☐ FREE

SIGHTS VISITED/ACTIVITIES

WILDLIFE

HIKES

☐
☐
☐

☐
☐
☐

OVERALL EXPERIENCE

DATE(S) VISITED

☐ FIRST VISIT   ☐ RETURN VISIT

PASSPORT STAMP

TRAVEL PARTNERS

LODGING

☐ RV   ☐ CABIN   ☐ TENT   ☐ DAY TRIP

WEATHER

FEE(S)

☐ FEE(S)   ☐ FREE

SIGHTS VISITED/ACTIVITIES

WILDLIFE

HIKES

☐
☐
☐

☐
☐
☐

OVERALL EXPERIENCE

DATE(S) VISITED

☐ FIRST VISIT   ☐ RETURN VISIT

PASSPORT STAMP

TRAVEL PARTNERS

LODGING

☐ RV   ☐ CABIN   ☐ TENT   ☐ DAY TRIP

WEATHER

FEE(S)

☐ FEE(S)   ☐ FREE

SIGHTS VISITED/ACTIVITIES

WILDLIFE

HIKES

☐
☐
☐

OVERALL EXPERIENCE

DATE(S) VISITED

☐ FIRST VISIT   ☐ RETURN VISIT

PASSPORT STAMP

TRAVEL PARTNERS

LODGING

☐ RV   ☐ CABIN   ☐ TENT   ☐ DAY TRIP

WEATHER

FEE(S)

☐ FEE(S)   ☐ FREE

SIGHTS VISITED/ACTIVITIES

WILDLIFE

HIKES

☐
☐
☐

☐
☐
☐

OVERALL EXPERIENCE

DATE(S) VISITED

☐ FIRST VISIT   ☐ RETURN VISIT

PASSPORT STAMP

TRAVEL PARTNERS

LODGING

☐ RV   ☐ CABIN   ☐ TENT   ☐ DAY TRIP

WEATHER

FEE(S)

☐ FEE(S)   ☐ FREE

SIGHTS VISITED/ACTIVITIES

WILDLIFE

HIKES

	☐
	☐
	☐

OVERALL EXPERIENCE

DATE(S) VISITED

☐ FIRST VISIT ☐ RETURN VISIT

PASSPORT STAMP

TRAVEL PARTNERS

LODGING

☐ RV ☐ CABIN ☐ TENT ☐ DAY TRIP

WEATHER

FEE(S)

☐ FEE(S) ☐ FREE

SIGHTS VISITED/ACTIVITIES

WILDLIFE

HIKES

☐
☐
☐

☐
☐
☐

OVERALL EXPERIENCE

DATE(S) VISITED

☐ FIRST VISIT   ☐ RETURN VISIT

PASSPORT STAMP

TRAVEL PARTNERS

LODGING

☐ RV   ☐ CABIN   ☐ TENT   ☐ DAY TRIP

WEATHER

FEE(S)

☐ FEE(S)   ☐ FREE

SIGHTS VISITED/ACTIVITIES

WILDLIFE

HIKES

☐
☐
☐
☐
☐
☐

OVERALL EXPERIENCE

DATE(S) VISITED

☐ FIRST VISIT ☐ RETURN VISIT

PASSPORT STAMP

TRAVEL PARTNERS

LODGING

☐ RV ☐ CABIN ☐ TENT ☐ DAY TRIP

WEATHER

FEE(S)

☐ FEE(S) ☐ FREE

SIGHTS VISITED/ACTIVITIES

WILDLIFE

HIKES

☐
☐
☐

☐
☐
☐

OVERALL EXPERIENCE

DATE(S) VISITED

☐ FIRST VISIT ☐ RETURN VISIT

PASSPORT STAMP

TRAVEL PARTNERS

LODGING

☐ RV ☐ CABIN ☐ TENT ☐ DAY TRIP

WEATHER

FEE(S)

☐ FEE(S) ☐ FREE

SIGHTS VISITED/ACTIVITIES

WILDLIFE

HIKES

☐
☐
☐

☐
☐
☐

OVERALL EXPERIENCE

DATE(S) VISITED

☐ FIRST VISIT   ☐ RETURN VISIT

PASSPORT STAMP

TRAVEL PARTNERS

LODGING

☐ RV   ☐ CABIN   ☐ TENT   ☐ DAY TRIP

WEATHER

FEE(S)

☐ FEE(S)   ☐ FREE

SIGHTS VISITED/ACTIVITIES

WILDLIFE

HIKES

☐
☐
☐
☐
☐
☐

OVERALL EXPERIENCE

Made in the USA
Monee, IL
29 May 2024

59076905R00056